Whatever Is Lovely

GUIDED JOURNAL

BELLE
CITY
GIFTS

Belle City Gifts
Savage, Minnesota, USA

Belle City Gifts is an imprint of BroadStreet Publishing Group LLC.
Broadstreetpublishing.com

Whatever Is Lovely (guided journal)

Design by Chris Garborg | garborgdesign.com
Compiled and edited by Michelle Winger | literallyprecise.com

Printed in China.

18   19   20   21   22   23   24   7   6   5   4   3   2   1

We don't see ourselves as capable enough to do anything in our own strength,
for our true competence flows from God's empowering presence.

2 Corinthians 3:5

If I could spend the day
any way I wanted, I would...

_____
_____
_____
_____
_____
_____
_____
_____
_____
_____
_____
_____
_____
_____
_____
_____
_____
_____
_____
_____
_____

He will watch over his lovers,
never letting them slip or be overthrown.

Psalm 55:22

Here are 20 things that make me smile

You don't have to be willing and able; you can just be willing because God is able.

One of the greatest moments
of my life was when...

He chose us to be his very own, joining us to himself
even before he laid the foundation of the universe!

Ephesians 1:4

A life of unconditional love looks like this

You're the only place of protection for me. I keep coming back to hide
myself in you, for you are like a mountain-cliff fortress where I am kept safe.

Psalm 71:3

Here are a few things
I couldn't live without

Respond gently when you are confronted
and you'll defuse the rage of another.

Proverbs 15:1

If I could go anywhere in the world, it would be...

Let your thoughts stretch above the canopy of everyday human details to bask in this joy: God has given you everything you need.

One thing that inspires me is

"What blessing comes to you when gentleness lives in you!
For you will inherit the earth."

Matthew 5:5

Here are a few things
I wish people knew about me

_____

_____

_____

_____

_____

_____

_____

_____

_____

_____

_____

_____

_____

_____

_____

_____

_____

_____

_____

_____

"Don't worry or surrender to your fear.
For if you've believed in God, now trust and believe in me also."

John 14:1

What has surprised me
most in life is...

_____

_____

_____

_____

_____

_____

_____

_____

_____

_____

_____

_____

_____

_____

_____

_____

_____

_____

_____

Make all of this your constant meditation and make it real with your life
so everyone can see that you are moving forward.

1 Timothy 4:15

Some things I'm learning to say no to are...

When you come to God
with your head hung low,
he lifts your chin,
looks warmly into your eyes,
and whispers tender words
of compassion that reach
the deepest place
in your heart.

I feel happiest when...

Surrender your anxiety!
Be silent and stop your striving and you will see that I am God.

Psalm 46:10

The people in my life who truly support me are...

Be cheerful with joyous celebration in every season of life.
Let joy overflow, for you are united with the Anointed One!

Philippians 4:4

These are the words
I need to hear

Everything we could ever need for life and complete devotion to God
has already been deposited in us by his divine power.

2 Peter 1:3

This is one of the most
satisfying jobs I've ever done

IT'S TEMPTING TO
TAKE SHORTCUTS,
BUT A LIFE OF
VICTORY DEMANDS
HARD WORK.

Here is something I am proud of

_____
_____
_____
_____
_____
_____
_____
_____
_____
_____
_____
_____
_____
_____
_____
_____
_____
_____
_____
_____

Watch your words and be careful what you say,
and you'll be surprised how few troubles you'll have.

I would really like
to learn more about...

_____
_____
_____
_____
_____
_____
_____
_____
_____
_____
_____
_____
_____
_____
_____
_____
_____
_____
_____
_____
_____

Send your kind mercy-kiss to comfort me, your servant,
just like you promised you would.

Psalm 119:76

My favorite Scripture is...

You are my only hope, Lord!
I've hung onto you, trusting in you all my life.

Psalm 71:5

The person I look up to
the most in life is...

_____

_____

_____

_____

_____

_____

_____

_____

_____

_____

_____

_____

_____

_____

_____

_____

_____

_____

_____

_____

_____

God's Word says that he makes all things beautiful in his time. Whatever situation you are facing right now has the potential to create beauty in you.

If I could meet anyone
in the world, it would be...

We come freely and boldly to where love is enthroned, to receive mercy's kiss and discover the grace we urgently need to strengthen us in our time of weakness.

Hebrews 4:16

My favorite time of the day is...

_____

_____

_____

_____

_____

_____

_____

_____

_____

_____

_____

_____

_____

_____

_____

_____

_____

_____

Cheer up! Take courage all you who love him.
Wait for him to break through for you, all who trust in him!

Psalm 31:24

One of my favorite
childhood memories is...

_____
_____
_____
_____
_____
_____
_____
_____
_____
_____
_____
_____
_____
_____
_____
_____
_____
_____
_____
_____
_____
_____
_____

We constantly pray that our God will empower you
to live worthy of all that he has invited you to experience.

2 Thessalonians 1:11

A tradition in my family that I love is...

_____
_____
_____
_____
_____
_____
_____
_____
_____
_____
_____
_____
_____
_____
_____
_____
_____
_____
_____

JOY FLOWS IN
THE MIDDLE OF
THE DARKNESS
AS YOU TRUST
IN GOD'S
PERFECT WAYS,
WHISPERING
THROUGH
YOUR TEARS,
"NOT MY WILL,
BUT YOURS
BE DONE."

My favorite place in the world is...

A man of deep understanding will give good advice,
drawing it out from the well within.

Spending some quiet time alone
makes me feel...

Brilliant ideas pay off and bring you prosperity,
but making hasty, impatient decisions will only lead to financial loss.

Something that made me
laugh out loud recently was...

Put your heart and soul into every activity you do,
as though you are doing if for the Lord himself and not merely for others.

Colossians 3:23

I feel most at peace when...

_____

_____

_____

_____

_____

_____

_____

_____

_____

_____

_____

_____

_____

_____

_____

_____

_____

_____

_____

_____

_____

_____

_____

Inspiration is an amazing circle. God gives vibrant colors, bursting flavors, comforting warmth, moving melodies, and unimaginable beauty, and your heart cannot help but respond in worship back to him.

If I could ask God one question,
it would be...

Discover creative ways to encourage others and to motivate them
toward acts of compassion, doing beautiful works as expressions of love.

One of the hardest things
I've ever had to do was...

Faith brings our hopes into reality and becomes the foundation needed to acquire the things we long for. It is the evidence required to prove what is still unseen.

Hebrews 11:1

My favorite day of the week is...

When we live our lives within the shadow of God Most High,
our secret hiding place, we will always be shielded from harm.

Psalm 91:9

I find it hard
to be patient when...

GOD WILL NOT
FAIL YOU WHEN
IT MATTERS MOST
OR IN THE
SMALL THINGS.
FAILURE IS NOT
POSSIBLE FOR GOD.

A story in the Bible that
captures my attention is...

Love never brings fear, for fear is always related to punishment.
But love's perfection drives the fear of punishment far from our hearts.

1 John 4:18

Here are three decisions
I need to make soon

God sends angels with special orders to protect you wherever you go,
defending you from all harm.

Psalm 91:11

Something that was
worth the wait for me was...

_____
_____
_____
_____
_____
_____
_____
_____
_____
_____
_____
_____
_____
_____
_____
_____
_____
_____
_____
_____

Lord, you are so good to me, so kind in every way
and ready to forgive, for your grace-fountain keeps overflowing,
drenching all your lovers who pray to you.

Psalm 86:5

I can't go anywhere without...

_____
_____
_____
_____
_____
_____
_____
_____
_____
_____
_____
_____
_____
_____
_____
_____
_____
_____
_____
_____
_____
_____

Your prayers, no matter how unintelligible they seem to you, are heard and understood by God. Your message is never lost in translation.

A characteristic I would love to possess is...

"If you embrace the truth, it will release more freedom into your lives."

John 8:32

I have worked
really hard to be...

The steps of the God-pursuing ones follow firmly in the footsteps of the Lord,
and God delights in every step they take to follow him.

Psalm 37:23

I want to be remembered
as someone who...

We are convinced that every detail of our lives is continually woven together
to fit into God's perfect plan of bringing good into our lives,
for we are his lovers who have been called to fulfill his designed purpose.

Romans 8:28

Here are ten things
I am grateful for today

GOLD, SILVER, SPARKLING JEWELS, DECADENCE, OPULENCE, SPLENDOR, IMMEASURABLE LOVE, JOY, PEACE, AND UNBROKEN RELATIONSHIP— IT'S YOUR INHERITANCE!

This is what makes me unique

Truthful words will stand the test of time,
but one day every lie will be seen for what it is.

This is how I've changed
in the last five years

_____

_____

_____

_____

_____

_____

_____

_____

_____

_____

_____

_____

_____

_____

_____

_____

_____

_____

_____

_____

In the midst of everything be always giving thanks,
for this is God's perfect plan for you in Christ Jesus.

My favorite season of the year is...

If anyone longs to be wise, ask God for wisdom and he will give it!

James 1:5

A typical day for me looks like this

Approach
the throne,
shamelessly
pull up a chair,
and lift your
voice to God.
He loves your
company.

Something I am hoping for is...

Let everyone thank God, for he is good, and he is easy to please!
His tender love for us continues on forever!

Psalm 136:1

I need the most grace for...

"I leave the gift of peace with you—my peace.
Not the kind of fragile peace given by the world, but my perfect peace.
Don't yield to fear or be troubled in your hearts—instead, be courageous!"

John 14:27

This is something I love
about where I live

_____

_____

_____

_____

_____

_____

_____

_____

_____

_____

_____

_____

_____

_____

_____

_____

_____

_____

_____

_____

I know that you delight to set your truth deep in my spirit.
So come into the hidden places of my heart and teach me wisdom.

Psalm 51:6

What I love
about my family is...

YOU ARE NOT A
WEAK SAPLING,
LIMITED BY
INADEQUATE LIGHT
AND MEAGER
NOURISHMENT.
YOU ARE A
STRONG AND
GRACEFUL OAK,
FLOURISHING AND
RESILIENT FOR THE
GLORY OF GOD.

Honoring my parents
looks like this

_____
_____
_____
_____
_____
_____
_____
_____
_____
_____
_____
_____
_____
_____
_____
_____
_____
_____
_____
_____
_____
_____
_____

May God, the inspiration and fountain of hope, fill you to overflowing
with uncontainable joy and perfect peace as you trust in him.

Romans 15:13

Here is something I
would love to do with my life

_____

_____

_____

_____

_____

_____

_____

_____

_____

_____

_____

_____

_____

_____

_____

_____

_____

_____

_____

_____

_____

_____

Laying your life down in tender surrender before the Lord
will bring life, prosperity, and honor as your reward.

Proverbs 22:4

I am especially thankful
for this today

_____

_____

_____

_____

_____

_____

_____

_____

_____

_____

_____

_____

_____

_____

_____

_____

_____

_____

_____

_____

_____

_____

_____

_____

Refusing constructive criticism shows you have no interest in improving your life.
For revelation-insight only comes as you accept correction
and the wisdom that it brings.

Proverbs 15:32

I find it difficult to
trust God in this area

Let no doubt take root;
God is a God who cares
deeply, loves fully,
and remains faithful —
ever at your side
in times of trouble.

Here is a story
I tell over and over

_____

_____

_____

_____

_____

_____

_____

_____

_____

_____

_____

_____

_____

_____

_____

_____

_____

_____

_____

_____

_____

_____

You draw near to those who call out to you,
listening closely, especially when their hearts are true.

Psalm 145:18

My creative outlet is...

"Behold, I'm standing at the door, knocking. If your heart is open to hear my voice and you open the door within, I will come in to you and feast with you, and you will feast with me."

Revelation 3:20

Something I find interesting about people is...

_____

_____

_____

_____

_____

_____

_____

_____

_____

_____

_____

_____

_____

_____

_____

_____

_____

_____

_____

_____

"Never forget that I am with you every day, even to the completion of this age."

Matthew 28:20

This is how I believe God sees me

_____

_____

_____

_____

_____

_____

_____

_____

_____

_____

_____

_____

_____

_____

_____

_____

_____

_____

_____

_____

_____

_____

Weakness isn't something to be feared or hidden; weakness submitted to God allows the power of Christ to work in and through you.

I feel most alive when...

Yes, he did mighty miracles and we are overjoyed!

Psalm 126:3

What hurts me most is...

Don't be pulled in different directions or worried about a thing.
Be saturated in prayer throughout each day,
offering your faith-filled requests before God with overflowing gratitude.

Philippians 4:6

This is my favorite psalm

Let the sunrise of your love end our dark night. Break through our clouded dawn again!
Only you can satisfy our hearts, filling us with songs of joy to the end of our days.

Psalm 90:14

I love reading about...

_____

_____

_____

_____

_____

_____

_____

_____

_____

_____

_____

_____

_____

_____

_____

_____

_____

_____

_____

_____

_____

_____

Hope starts with the promises of God.

Here is an experience that
made me feel deeply loved

"You can ask and keep on asking him!
And you can be sure that you'll receive what you ask for,
and your joy will have no limits!"

John 16:24

A proverb I live by is...

_____
_____
_____
_____
_____
_____
_____
_____
_____
_____
_____
_____
_____
_____
_____
_____
_____
_____
_____
_____
_____

Walk holy, in a way that is suitable to your high rank,
given to you in your divine calling.

Ephesians 4:1-2

This is where I go
when I need to get away

Don't allow your hearts to grow dull or lose your enthusiasm,
but follow the example of those who fully received what God had promised
because of their strong faith and patient endurance.

Hebrews 6:12

If I could change one thing
about myself, it would be...

BREATHE
IN THIS FRESH START: TODAY IS A NEW DAY, FULL OF PROMISE AND
LIFE.

Here's something unusual that happened to me recently

This is the one who gives his strength and might to his people.
This is the Lord giving us his kiss of peace.

Psalm 29:11

I highly value this

We've kept you always in our prayers that you would receive
the perfect knowledge of God's pleasure over your lives.

Colossians 1:9

I feel the most embraced
by God's presence when...

_____
_____
_____
_____
_____
_____
_____
_____
_____
_____
_____
_____
_____
_____
_____
_____
_____
_____
_____
_____
_____
_____

If your faith remains strong, even while surrounded by life's difficulties,
you will continue to experience the untold blessings of God!

James 1:12

This is how I receive love

_____

_____

_____

_____

_____

_____

_____

_____

_____

_____

_____

_____

_____

_____

_____

_____

_____

_____

_____

_____

_____

_____

_____

_____

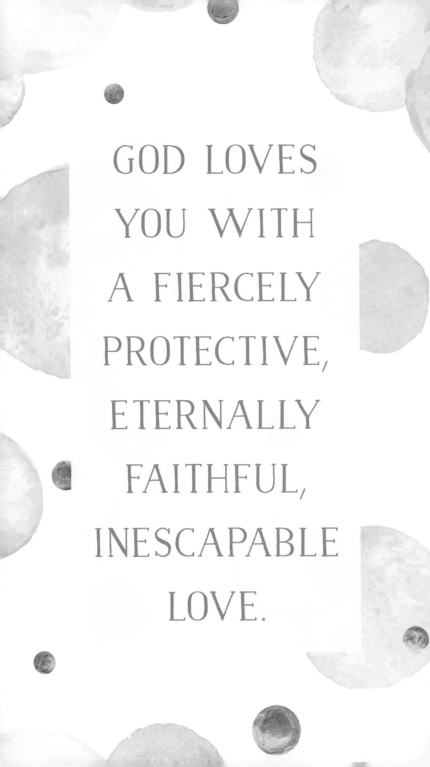

GOD LOVES
YOU WITH
A FIERCELY
PROTECTIVE,
ETERNALLY
FAITHFUL,
INESCAPABLE
LOVE.

I show my love for others by...

When it seems as though you are facing nothing but difficulties,
see it as an invaluable opportunity to experience the greatest joy that you can!

James 1:2–3

This is how I
serve other people

"You will be satisfied with a full life and with all that I do for you.
For you will enjoy the fullness of my salvation!"

Psalm 91:16

My favorite parable is...

Lord, I have chosen you alone as my inheritance.
You are my prize, my pleasure, and my portion.
I leave my destiny and its timing in your hands.

Psalm 16:5

My priorities in life
right now are...

God is faithful
to the deepest needs
of your heart;
he knows you
full well!

Something that fascinates me about God's creation is...

Don't lose your bold, courageous faith, for you are destined for a great reward!

Hebrews 10:35

Here's something that changed my life significantly

Be assured that anything you do that is beautiful and excellent
will be repaid by our Lord, whether you are an employee or an employer.

Ephesians 6:8

One of the biggest transformations
I've been through is...

_____
_____
_____
_____
_____
_____
_____
_____
_____
_____
_____
_____
_____
_____
_____
_____
_____
_____
_____
_____

Whom have I in heaven but you? You're all I want!
No one on earth means as much to me as you.

Psalm 73:25

Here's a list of things
I want to pray for regularly

Your best line
of defense is to
surround yourself
with the truth.
Read it. Think it.
Pray it. Declare it.

Something I really need
God's guidance for right now is

Praise God for his astonishing gift, which is far too great for words!

2 Corinthians 9:15

One of the things I love the most about God's character is

_____

_____

_____

_____

_____

_____

_____

_____

_____

_____

_____

_____

_____

_____

_____

_____

_____

_____

_____

_____

_____

Let your heart always be guided by the peace of the Anointed One,
who called you to peace as part of his one body. And always be thankful.

Colossians 3:15

Something new I learned
from God's Word recently is...

The wisdom from above is always pure, filled with peace, considerate and teachable. It is filled with love and never displays prejudice or hypocrisy in any form.

James 3:17

A fear I need to face is...

THE TRUTH OF GOD'S LOVE IS OVERWHELMING: WHEN SUCH DEVOTION HAS BEEN PROVEN, WHAT ELSE COULD ATTRACT YOUR GAZE?

This is how journaling has helped me